SMALL POOLS

SMALL POOLS

Fanny Tagavi

HDi

Harper
DESIGN
international

An Imprint of HarperCollins*Publishers*

SMALL POOLS, revised edition
Copyright © 2004 by LOFT and HDI, an imprint of HarperCollins*Publishers*

First published in 2001 by:
HBI, an imprint of HarperCollins*Publishers*
10 East 53rd Street New York, NY 10022

Distributed throughout the world by:
HarperCollins International
10 East 53rd Street
New York, NY 10022
Fax: (212) 207-7654

HarperCollins books may be purchased for educational, business, or sales promotional use. For
information, please write: Special Markets Department, Harper Collins Publishers Inc., 10 East 53rd Street
New York, NY 10022

Editor: Paco Asensio

Text: Fanny Tagavi

Photographs: Pere Planells

Art Director: Mireia Casanovas Soley

Graphic Design: Emma Termes Parera

Translation: Wendy Griswold

Proofreading: Julie King

Printed in Spain

Anman Gràfiques del Vallès, Spain

D.L.: 17898-2004

Library of Congress Cataloging-in-Publication Data

Tagavi, Fanny, 1962-
  [Pequeñas piscinas con encanto. English]
  Small pools/edited by Paco Asensio ; [photography by Pere Planells]. -- Rev. ed.
      p. cm.
  Text by Fanny Tagavi and translation by Wendy Griswold.
  ISBN 0-06-056758-9 (pbk.)
    1. Swimming pools. 2. Architecture, Domestic. 3. Architectural photography. I. Asensio
Cerver, Francisco. II. Planells, Pere. III. Title.

TH4763.T2813 2003
728'.962--dc21

                                                              2003047808

If you would like to suggest projects for inclusion in future volumes, please email details to us at:
loft@loftpublications.com

We have tried our best to contact all copyright holders. In individual cases where this has not been possible,
we request copyright holders to get in touch with the publishing house.

First printing, 2004

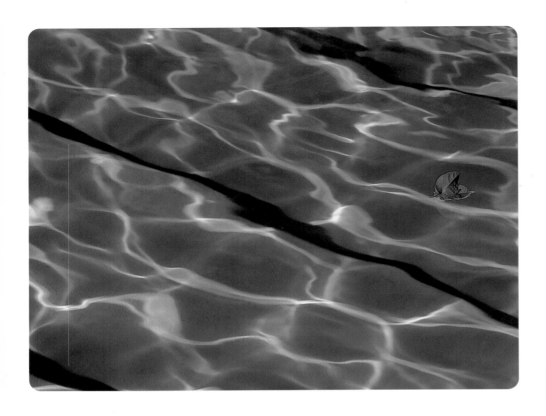

The term "pool" once meant a tub of water that could function as a storage tank, a fish hatchery, or, as we know it today, as a place to swim. To discover the origins of pools, we must go back to Roman times. In the Roman house, one type of pool was the *impluvium*, a decorative basin that collected rainwater. In Roman cities near the sea, another pool was the *vivarium*, where fish intended for consumption were kept. As the *limaria*, the pool formed part of an aqueduct system for collecting and distributing water. Finally, and only in the *thermae*, the public bathing complexes of Roman cities, we find the first swimming pool, the *natorium*, shaped like a cistern. Another type of pool, the garden pool, became common in the early seventeenth century, with the arrival of the baroque style, and lasted until the nineteenth century. The garden pools purpose was mainly aesthetic: it provided visual and auditory enjoyment for the pedestrian seeking a source of reflection and inspiration in a domestic setting. Thus, the usage and meaning of the word "pool" has evolved slowly since antiquity, until it finally came to be known as it is today, whether elegant, therapeutic, or simply recreational.

There has been one constant, parallel element in the historical development of the pool, the *thermae*, among the oldest therapeutic systems in the world, which, according to some research, date back to the second century BC with the construction of the Stabian Baths of Pompeii, the oldest still in existence. *Thermae* and public baths nearly disappeared when obscurantism arrived in central Europe in the Middle Ages and the Church spoke out against the ritual of the bath by proclaiming that spiritual purity took priority over physical cleanliness. Meanwhile, in the rest of Europe, and in Islamic and Middle Eastern societies, social, hygienic, and religious baths flourished. Architecturally, they consisted of a large central space with vaulted ceilings, heated by steam and surrounded by smaller rooms, decorated with marble or mosaics. Despite the passage of time and certain vicissitudes, the *hammam* has not only survived, but has become common, even in sports complexes. Because of their ability to stimulate genuine physical and psychological well-being, we have included the designs of several *hammams* that have integrated the thermal bath and in which water, as a source of health, plays the starring role.

Over the years, the pool, as a piece of construction, has evolved in accordance with architectural trends. But it was only in the mid-twentieth century, with the development of new materials and construction methods, that designers have been able to give free reign to their boundless imaginations, creating, shaping, and molding an environment. Hence, the richness of the projects presented in this book all share a growing concern for the disappearance of ecological balance. This concern translates into a great respect for the natural spaces where the water areas have been integrated. The projects in this book merge perfectly with their surroundings, as a tribute to nature's generosity.

Humankind's creativity has made it possible to enter the transparent fluidity of a sheet of turquoise water that peeks out over a cliff; to seemingly connect with infinity by transforming a recess in an old quarry into a pool and luxuriant garden; or to simply recapture ancient eastern customs and practices. Materials, textures, shapes, and colors merge in a magnificent exercise in cultural and social architecture that cannot fail to impress. Architecture and emotion have always joined together to realize the human being's instinct for perfection.

—Fanny Tagavi

Between a small field and an orchard of young fruit trees, this swimming pool, located in Palma de Mallorca, Spain, is framed by a border of rocks on which the patina of time has left its mark. Three mysterious steps invite the onlooker to enter the transparent fluidity of the water.

This project wisely used the elements of the country house to visually connect the pool area on different levels, similar to a three-dimensional picture. The original stones from the country home were used to divide the principal space into three areas: the swimming pool, the ancient mill, and a sunbathing zone on the upper level.

The old Z-shaped retaining wall becomes a path and shelters the pool, which was originally a reservoir that collected water to irrigate the field. The small, tidy orchard still stretches, on a second level, to the foot of the pool, along with the remains of a small treadmill, now a sculpture for contemplation, a silent witness to the past.

RECOVERING THE PAST

Location: **Majorca, Spain**
Surface area: **129 sq. ft.**

A panorama of the two areas that comprise the main level: the swimming pool and the old mill. On the second level orchard of young fruit trees stands.

The pool, formerly a reservoir, is complemented by the charm of the nearby fruit trees.

This ancient reservoir, restored and converted into a swimming pool, is sheltered by a 200-year-old wall and is perfectly integrated with the original structure of the house. The pool's charm comes from the bewitching turquoise color of its water and the ocher luminosity of the ancient wall that borders one side of the pool.

To blend the pool's profile into setting, a sandstone trim was chosen, whose sand-like color complements the rest of the materials used. On one end, a small retaining wall, also covered with stones, functions as an informal diving board or sunbathing area. Behind it, lush vegetation flourishes, hiding a stone guest house from view.

The ends of the pool are characterized by very diverse landscaping: at one end is the color and splendor of freely-growing vegetation; the other, the precision and simplicity of a monastic cloister. The two landscape treatments are joined by a path with rounded edges, which runs rectilinear and parallel to the pool and sharply interrupts the green grass of a small orchard of fruit trees.

At the end of the path, a few steps down, a fountain offers passersby the coolness and musicality of its crystalline waters. These details were created to delight and soothe the senses through the power of nature's beauty and simplicity.

BETWEEN TWO WORLDS

Location: **Tuscany, Italy**
Surface area: **161 sq. ft.**

This rectangular pool is protected by a 200-year-old wall. At the back, a low retaining wall serves as a diving board.

The inside of the pool is coated with green gresite, so the water takes on a magnificent turquoise color which highlights the luminous ocher color of the ancient wall that shelters it.

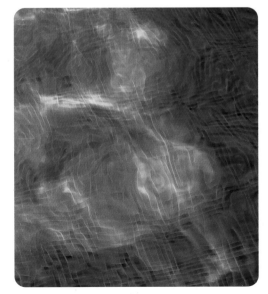

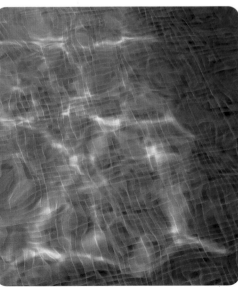

The vegetation that grows freely at one end of the pool hides a stone guest house.

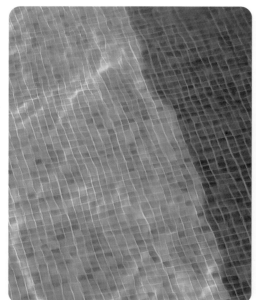

A path with rounded edges, running rectilinear and parallel to the pool, interrupts the green grass of a small orchard of fruit trees.

Amid rocks cracked by the sun, rural fragrances, and the buzz of grasshoppers, a smooth slope shelters low stone

A STREAM AMID THE ROCKS

Location: **Ibiza, Spain**
Surface area: **269 sq. ft.**

walls that were once used for terrace farming, a traditional system of agriculture. At the foot of the slope lies the emerald water of this pool, which combines artificial curves and rough shapes.

The designer of this project applied architectural criteria to the natural setting and achieved a perfect blending of both. Any landscaping around the pool was rejected in order to maintain the strength of the earth and rock, in stark contrast to the soft luminosity of the water. In accordance with this goal, the land needed for the pool was cleared, and the exterior perimeter was covered with a simple, wide stone strip.

The rocky side of the pool has a small platform that serves as a lounging area and natural diving board. A small, completely whitewashed well that provides fresh water is at the side of the pool. The gentle slope serves as an informal entrance to the pool, which is reinforced by the presence of steps in the shape of waves submerged in the water.

In this place of light and contrast, the priority was to preserve the appearance of the landscape; thus the setting had to remain the star player.

The originality of this pool lies in the preservation of the surrounding terrain into the project. The pool was blended into the setting, creating a pool shaped like a natural pond. A whitewashed well that provides fresh water overlooks the pool.

The contrast between the emerald color of the water and the ocher of the rock reinforces the sensation of being at a streambed.

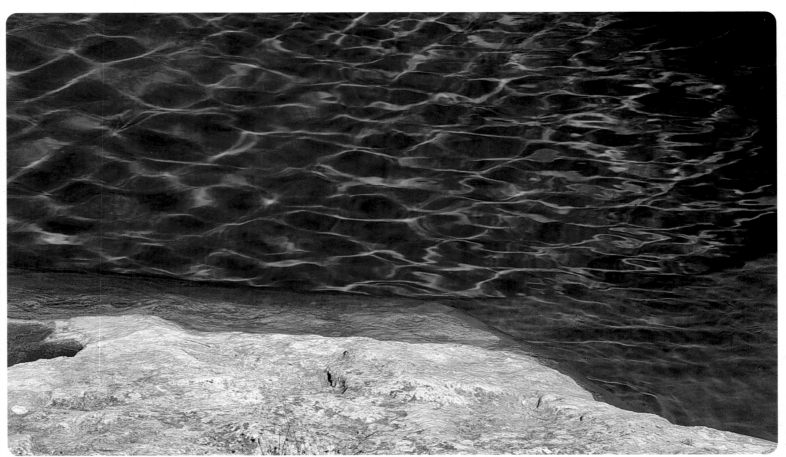

This rectangular pool sits between two long, stone dividing walls and is surrounded by a soft tapestry of grass. The

RURAL SYMMETRY

Location: **Santorini, Greece**
Surface area: **258 sq. ft.**

principal goal of the design was to overcome the problems presented by the site, a narrow band surrounded by walls of varying heights. Therefore, the site's sharp linearity had to be compensated for and smaller areas had to be created on the two shorter sides, where the presence of low and medium-high walls physically and visually prevented any expansion.

To break the rigidity of the straight lines and to add volume, the principal and older wall was used as support for dense vegetation that could spread out like a natural cascade. This vegetation, comprised mainly of a spectacular bougainvillea and various common plant species, softens the harshness of the dry stone and iso-

lates this area, ensuring a peaceful, intimate setting. A limestone rim puts the finishing touch on this sheet of calm water and houses the ingenious channels that return water to the pool in order to prevent the carpet of grass from flooding.

One end, located at the entrance to the open area, became an informal porch extending from a rear wall. A unique canopy makes this angular spot a pleasant niche, perfectly integrated into the space. On the opposite end, three steps break up the dividing wall while joining the two side walls. This solution, using only one material, stone, made it possible to construct a formal area for sunbathing. Several stylized lounges of tropical wood complete the setting and add a note of color.

Detail of the ocher canopy at the entrance to the open space. This pleasant corner, which serves as an informal porch extending from a rear wall, is carpeted with the same soft grass that covers the entire area.

The pool is located on a narrow strip of land surrounded by dividing walls of varying heights. The dense vegetation that spreads out over the dry stone adds volume and breaks up the formal linearity.

The placement and magnificent orientation of this swimming pool were two determining factors in this project, treated as a sheet of still water that engages in a dialogue with its surroundings. The overall effect is of the depth like an infinite mirror between the earth and sky.

The irregularly-shaped swimming pool, bordered with small peninsulas of rock, resembles a calm nat-ural lake, a niche where one can find peace and primordial silence. In one of the corners, melting into the land-scape, a tree trunk is visible, twisted by the passage of time and placed strategically for contemplation in accor-dance with the tenets of Zen philosophy. In this respect, the designers wanted to avoid overloading the space around the swimming pool, preferring to give a starring role to the splendid natural surroundings.

This infinity pool is edged with the same type of rock used for the small artificial peninsulas. The rocks accentuate the natural, integrated feeling by avoiding a continuous, defined edge. The swimming pool was not intended to change the landscape, but to be a continuation of it. So the materials for the pool and the various areas surrounding the water are unified. These are at the same level as the water's surface, strengthening the visual continuity and the spectacular character of the landscape, which blends seamlessly with the main level of the swimming pool.

A MIRROR BETWEEN THE EARTH AND SKY

Location: **Majorca, Spain**
Surface area: **430 sq. ft.**

A key factory in integrating the pool naturally into its surroundings was unifying the materials as well as the different zones around the pool.

The twisted trunk of a tree that shows the passage of time is situated in a strategic position where it merges with the landscape. The tree obliges the onlooker to stop and contemplate it, in accordance with the guidelines of Zen philosophy.

The small rock peninsulas and the unified use of materials in the surrounding area give the pool the sensation of being a natural water pond.

The beautiful perspective offered by the site´s orientation influenced the decision to treat this pool like a static sheet of water.

A small pond in the exotic intimacy of an interior Moroccan patio, this shallow pool is another example of how mosaics are still used in Morocco.

Traditional inspiration

An elaborate, bright turquoise finish that acquires all its splendor from the sun's reflection crowns a bright border that extends around the entire interior perimeter of the pool. A soft salmon color covers the patio, creating a chromatic axis between the pool and the principal and side façades, which also boast Moroccan floor tiles and two magnificent wooden chairs that preside over the pool like thrones. At a higher level, steps covered in gresite the same color as the pool lead to a small terrace dominated by three arched windows. Wrought iron and wood furnishings decorate a breakfast/dinner nook with elegant simplicity.

This is a dynamic space, conceived for intimacy, with a design based on Moroccan decorative tradition, in which even the simplicity of a border stands out as a complex geometric exercise. Color and textures merge here to create a unique, formal, balanced, and aesthetically pleasing space.

Location: **Douar Abiat, Morocco**
Surface area: **108 sq. ft.**

An elaborate, bright turquoise finish that derives all its splendor from the sun's reflection crowns a plain border that extends around the entire interior perimeter of the pool.

The lateral façade houses a small space paved with Moroccan tiles and decorated with two magnificent wooden chairs.

A cool, peaceful refuge, this small oasis emerges from the arid land that surrounds it. A geometric balance comes from the perfect relationship of its three volumes: the swimming pool, rectilinear and with a smooth surface of water; the terrace; and the main building; both just one story high. A stone wall of medium height, perfectly restored, joins the two structures and at the same time surrounds the entire property.

The visual perspective from the fence is the same at any point, since the property and the adjacent land are at the same level. The intent was to bring out a play of contrasts resulting from the juxtaposition of the dry land and the artificial grass that surrounds the blue surface of the water.

A sense of continuity comes from the homogeneousness of the colors and the materials used to restore the property and build the pool. The stone and the sand color become the chromatic base of the setting, heightening the awareness of the intense blue of the water and green of the vegetation.

The only vertical element, two regal palm trees, stand between the two main buildings, dominating the pool area and breaking the infinite immensity of the sky. The evocative presence of these palms, as in a desert oasis, acts as a guide from the road.

COLOR CONTRASTS

Location: **Majorca, Spain**
Surface area: **516 sq. ft.**

The patio, where a granary originally stood, opens up onto the pool at the same level. The barbecue area can be seen next to the sofa.

Detail of the bench inside the pool, which extends from one side to the other.

The perimeter of the pool was built with natural stone of the same sand color as the wall that surrounds the property. The predominance of straight lines enhances the contrasting colors while making the pool a fluid mirror, perfectly integrated with the surroundings.

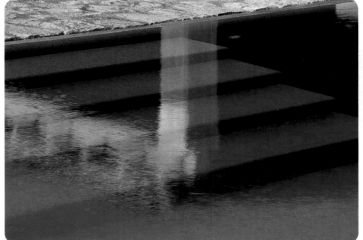

The only decorative elements are wooden chaise longues whose refined style is enhanced by the whiteness of the cushions.

This magnificent, colorful pool, surrounded by a dense wall of vegetation, blends perfectly with its natural surroundings.

THE REINTERPRETATION
OF WATER

Location: **Marrakech, Morocco**
Surface area: **430 sq. ft.**

A spectacular stepped entrance invites the visitor to slip into the therapeutic pleasure of the water and enjoy the beauty of the landscape from a wide underwater bench.

The intense color of this pool, bright and cheerful, combined with the complex geometry of the double edging of fired clay that finishes off the edges, is an example of the craftsmanship still practiced today in Marrakech, where the property is located. The excellent glazed mosaic work on the central band of the small channel that bisects the edging and the various geometric finishes located both inside and outside the pool are small sam-

plings of the ornamental richness that has characterized this country for centuries.

At one end of the pool, symmetrically aligned at ground level, six slender jets of water form a unique fountain, that is an integral part of the project. Details, sounds, colors, and textures merge here to create an inviting world, one with the strength and personality of a thousand-year-old architectural culture.

On the grass, beneath the thick foliage of the trees, two contemporary white chairs in the shape of butterflies invite guests to contemplate this mysterious and magical place.

Behind the water fountain, on the carpet of grass, there is a glimpse of the past in the form of an ancient fired clay vessel. The entire pool is surrounded by a thick carpet of grass that comes right up to the edge.

The water jets at ground level are integrated with the rest of the pool. Under the water, the special treatment applied to the ceramic floor tiles to separate the fountain area from the pool area is clearly evident.

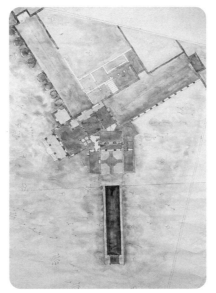

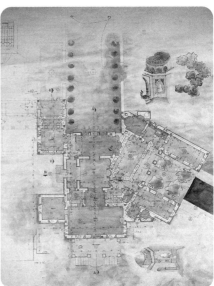

Two drawings show the landscape architect's original design for the project.

The double edging of fired clay reflects a geometric exercise that is characteristic of this country's architectural traditions.

The stepped entrance to the pool invites the visitor to slip into the water and enjoy the beauty of the landscape from an underwater bench.

Inspired by Versailles, this swimming pool imitates the suggestive shapes of the lush gardens at the French royal palace.

THE ETERNAL CYCLE OF WATER

However, it has a trait all its own: an ingenious system of channels surrounding a small island where six olive trees grow. There is continuous movement of water, since this area is connected to a pond on a lower level. This keeps the swimming pool clean, converts a retaining wall into a charming waterfall, and adds the relaxing sound of running water. At night, an arbor that serves as an informal patio is a magical area for dining, enjoying a drink, or just chatting.

The pool is perfectly symmetrical, its linearity broken only by two semicircles. The first forms the island and the second, directly across from it, contains underwater steps.

The size of the garden has been strictly respected, both on the upper and lower levels. The olive and palm trees, freely spreading their exotic beauty, are the stars of this orchard.

This project integrates the entire setting. It employs a refined, almost stark style, which emphasizes the central axis created by the pool as well as the setting itself, creating many perspectives, such as the one framed by the columns of the arbor.

Location: **Majorca, Spain**
Surface area: **484 sq. ft.**

From this angle the two levels can be seen: the water is the link between them.
Bougainvillea dots the immense garden with a variety of warm colors.

The location of the arbor provides a restful, shady area. The pool was shaped using natural slip-proof stone, which was also used for the columns supporting the arbor.

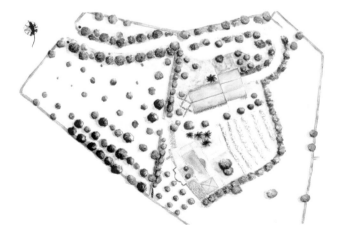

A drawing of the garden and the water area.

A view of the olive trees, perfectly integrated with the pool and the setting through an ingenious system of channels surrounding the island they grow on. The visual continuity between the group of trees and the landscape that softly envelops it can be appreciated from any angle.

Four wide steps invite guests into the water. Low, natural stone walls surround the pool and house areas. A rustic shower emerges from the foliage of an indigenous tree.

High and low walls mark the different levels as well as the various landscaped areas surrounding the house and pool. A combination of open and more secluded spaces was chosen to enhance the setting's natural beauty.

In a magnificent Marrakech palm grove, one can make out the unique silhouette of this house, protected by a high sand-colored wall which, among other things, shields the landscaped area and main building from the harshness of the sun. Inside, different levels extend from the central interior patio, as is the custom in this culture.

Starting from the patio, the architectural rhythm of the house and exterior areas is presented as a series of discontinuous spaces that create amazing perspectives which can be enjoyed from anywhere in the house.

The pool area is surrounded by a multicolored garden where palm trees, yuccas, climbers, fragrant plants, and various fruit trees are responsible for the special microclimate of this space, which is very cool during the summer. A soft carpet of grass covers the garden right up to one side of the pool.

On the opposite side, a green mosaic covers the strip between the pool and the garden wall, unifying all the colors on the ground. A restrained geometric border in elegant tones, the only note of color in this decidedly herbaceous setting, decorates the upper edges and the top of the inner perimeter.

IN THE SHADE OF
A PALM GROVE

Location: **Douar Abiat, Morocco**
Surface area: **108 sq. ft.**

A restrained geometric border in elegant tones, the only note of artificial color in this setting, decorates the upper edges of the pool and the top of the inner perimeter.

The pool is surrounded by a garden that features a wide range of indigenous vegetation. The garden creates its own microclimate that protects it from the heat.

A stylized iron chair in the shape of a fish casts its shadow on a wall, sand colored like the inside of the pool.

A typical Moroccan wooden door, studded and painted in a soft turquoise, connects the main building with the recreation area.

With elegant simplicity, this unique pool seems to slow the passage of time, which is almost halted in this space dedicated to contemplation and beauty. Two levels of water are enhanced by an elaborate garden that softens the melancholy of the stone, which has been faded and polished by the indelible mark of man and time.

Surrounded by a delicate iron railing, which sometimes disappears amid the vegetation, the pool area is comprised of two surfaces on different levels connected by a stone channel. The upper level, an ancient reservoir, is connected by an old system of water channels to the lower level, which is actually the main pool.

A magnificent pergola bordered by thick hedges marks the center of this composition and visually defines the two spaces. In the middle, as if spouting from the earth itself, a peaceful jet of water murmurs tirelessly inside a perfect circle of stone located mid-way between the two levels. With the singular familiarity of a sundial, the fountain enhances the geometry of the pergola, which surrounds and protects it.

To strengthen the composition, the ground was completely paved with cobblestones of varying shades of gray that sparkle when caressed by the sun.

CARVED
IN STONE

Location: **Mollégés, France**
Surface area: **322 sq. ft.**

Detail of the central fountain that joins the two levels. The entire area is paved with cobblestones of varying shades of gray.

The main pool is enclosed by a solid border of rustic stone with two symmetrical rows of clay flowerpots filled with cheerful red geraniums.

A view of the main pool's outlet, where a pile of river rocks acts as a natural filter, blocking leaves and other debris.

This semi-overflowing swimming pool, surrounded and protected by a luxuriant forest of Mediterranean pine, is situated below the house's main level. Connected by a simple path of natural stone, the presence of the water is announced in a sudden explosion of blue among the dry, fragrant pines.

At the end of the path, a broad, smooth slope reminiscent of typical Mediterranean fishing wharves is an invitation to plunge into the coolness of the turquoise water. The lively tonality was achieved by coating the inside of the pool in a light tone—a simple way to achieve bright, colorful effects by means of a contrast with the natural greens.

Surrounded with a broad edging of cream-colored artificial stone, the perimeter of the pool combines straight lines and soft curves, creating a totally balanced volume, in contrast to the architectonic lines of the house. The irregular shape of the pool, the elevation of the land, and the line of overflowing water not only lend personality and character to this composition, but also offer interesting visual perspectives, since the pool is at treetop level.

The overflow area was created in response to both aesthetic and functional concerns: this system makes it easy to maintain the pool because the water's movement clears away the needles falling from the surrounding pines.

Almost at the level of the water, the slender figures of weather-beaten tree trunks frame the entrance to the pool, standing like symbolic, welcoming sentinels.

THE COLOR TURQUOISE

Location: **Ibiza, Spain**
Surface area: **408 sq. ft.**

Peaceful and filled with color, the pool lies below the house. Its balanced volume was created to contrast with the house's architectural rigidity. In the photo on the left, the ramp inspired by typical Mediterranean fishing wharves can be seen.

The line of overflowing water seemingly blends the pool with the pines that surround and protect it. On a second level, the horizon line and the blue color of the sea can be seen.

The location of the swimming pool, below the house and surrounded by a dense pine forest, affords plenty of privacy.

This splendid garden, which extends generously to the east and west of the property, was conceived as a succession of individual spaces united by an imaginary straight line. On one side, this line takes the form of a channel of water, and on the other, it blends with the green hues of the grass that covers the entrance to the rear gardens.

Four formal gardens extend from the central point of the magnificent restored house, which is painted a vanilla color, extend four classical gardens. Two of the gardens include conceptually different pools: one for visual amusement, and the other for swimming. The studied landscaping invites reflection in a visitor strolling through the succession of different spaces, each lovingly landscaped and united by their classical features and visual perspectives.

The area opposite the porch, previously the site of a dismal metal sheep shed, now contains a serene pond which reflects the warm light of Provence and the shadow of a stand of unyielding plane trees. A series of massive spheres, the eternal symbol of perfection, are carved out of solid rock and align themselves with balanced precision on ancient bases in front of the pond.

Another highlight is the stylized Aeolian fountain, also in the form of a circle of vegetation, from which crystalline water flows. Fish, ducks, and frogs inhabit this water area, which is covered by water lilies in velvet tones. A channel of water flows from the pond and extends between a long line of olive and cypress trees, terminating some 262 feet later in a small pool shaped like a half moon, surrounded by iris and willows.

CLASSICAL SPIRIT

Location: **Saint-Rémy de Pce., France**
Surface area: **129 sq. ft.**

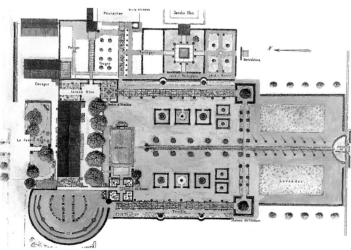

The silhouettes of the plane trees, planted to provide shade, are reflected in the pond, opposite the porch.

Although conceived as individual elements in a sequence, the spaces are united by a straight waterway edged by a long line of olive and cypress trees.

One color, white jade, and a single material, a clay-like stone from a quarry, are the two key elements that serve as a

MINIMALIST
CHARACTER

Location: Miami, Florida, USA
Surface area: **150 sq. ft.**

thread between the main building and the pool to produce a homogeneous architectural volume. In fact, when viewed from one of the side walls that shelter the house's winter porch, the pool becomes a logical extension of the house.

To accentuate the integration of both spaces, the pool was structured on two levels that merge into one: the level that starts at the winter porch, where three large windows shaped like sliding doors open up, and another that starts at the summer porch, where the stairs to the pool are located. Thus, the water does not just surround the interior and exterior recreation areas, but becomes a calm, restrained, modern pool with a highly refined style.

The ubiquitous white stone, which surrounds the

property like a protective cloak, embellishes the house, and adds an element of surprise due to its unique clay-like texture and smooth luminosity, which highlight the linearity of the grouping and add a certain dynamism. To keep with this approach, the summer porch was paved with the same material, so the pool is strongly connected with this exterior area. A thin netting, manipulated by means of a sophisticated mechanism, serves as a minimalist canopy in an area intended for sunbathing during the day and as a summer porch at night.

As for the garden, its elegant, green grass brings out the luminosity of the stone. At the main entrance to the house, a pine tree more than 50 years old welcomes visitors and is the only vertical element in a garden that prefers to spotlight the architectural work.

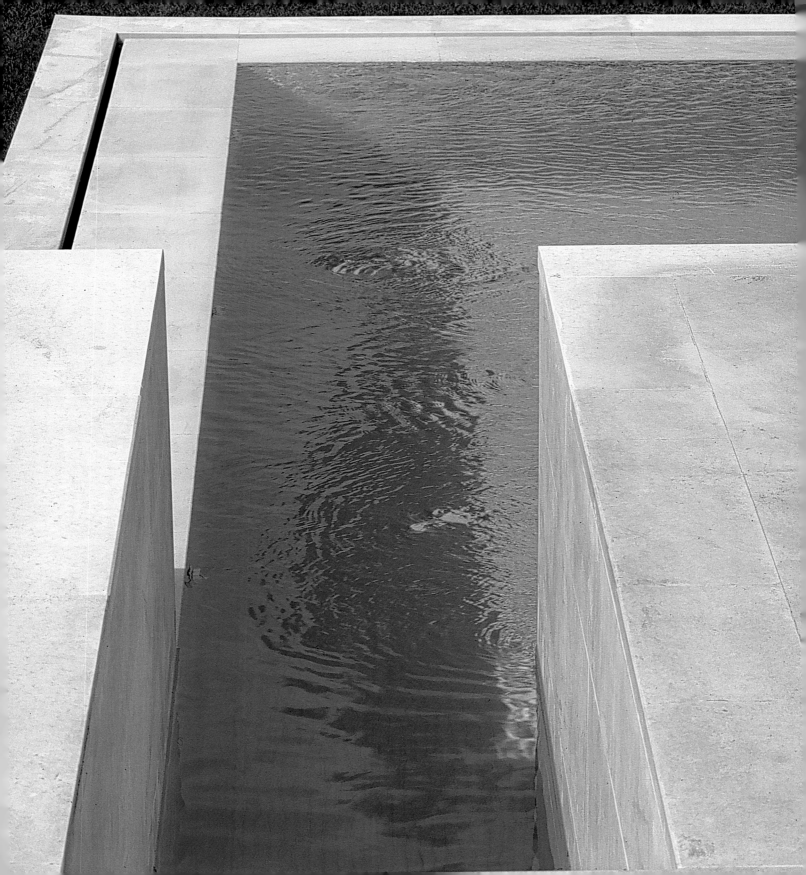

Opposite the luminous summer porch is the entrance to the pool, a narrow stairway between two wide, low walls that function as a solid banister. The pool was built of the same clay-like material used for the house.

A detail of the horizontal opening that provides light to the underground garage. At the back, the water glides over the low wall in a flat cascade.

Refined and almost monastic, this swimming pool recaptures the spirit of the Roman thermae, the ancient public

PRIVATE SPACE

baths known for their importance as social centers. But here the aesthetic of the Roman civilization has been replaced by an austere, restrained style that comes to life only with the caress of sunlight.

Built as an independent structure attached to the main dwelling, the pool is sheltered from the wind by three high, intensely white walls. Palm trees and pine trees surrounding the house peek over the walls. The pool's rectangular shape occupies almost the entire space, leaving just a narrow strip that functions as both ornamental trim and walkway.

The continuity of the white color enhances the balance of the composition. A chromatic contrast is accentuated through the use of the color indigo, at the client's request, to coat the pool's interior. Throughout the day, the play of light and shadow imparts volume and geometry to the area. At nightfall, the heat accumulated during the daylight hours keeps the water warm.

In addition to providing physical pleasure, this unique pool is also an intimate, private space, ideal for meditation.

Location: **Ibiza, Spain**
Surface area: **54 sq. ft.**

The work's linearity offers bright, colorful, geometric perspectives, such as the one that can be enjoyed from the entrance. A narrow strip of blue color frames the water, giving it visual depth.

Access to the pool is via two built-in steps. Levels and gradients are geometrically balanced by the continuity of the white paint.

Beyond the twisted trunk of an old carob tree, the different levels of the pool are visible. The key to its formal balance lies in the restrained style and two-color minimalism.

Three tall walls painted in an intense white shelter the pool from the wind. The tops of the pine and palm trees that surround the house can be seen from the pool.

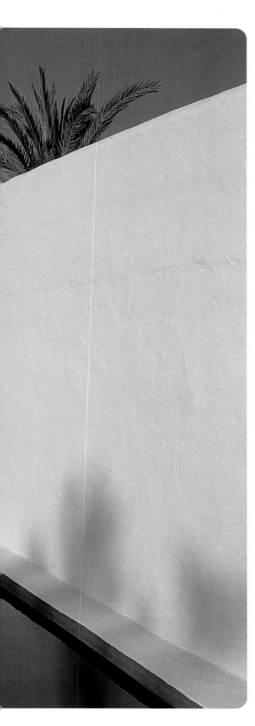

Throughout the day, the light creates different shadows that impart volume and geometry to this austere space.

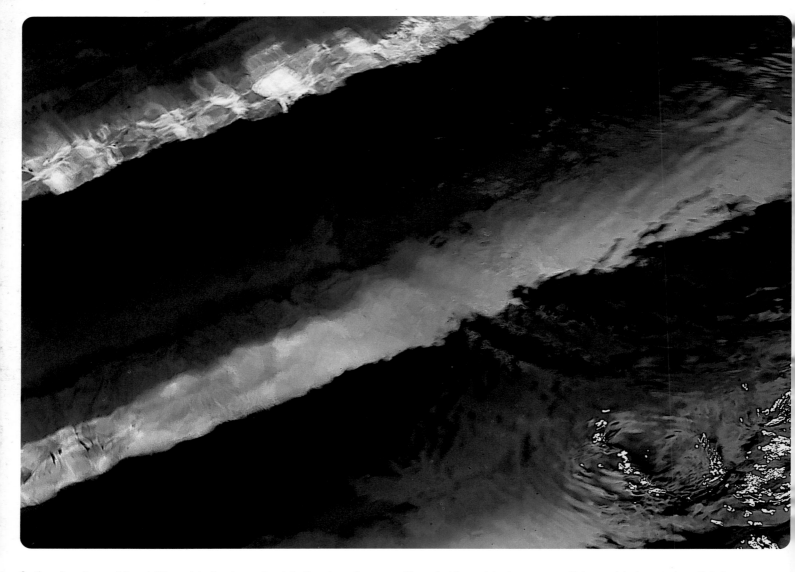

On the edge of a small forest, this pool, in the shape of an irrigation channel, emerges like a placid mountain river. The quiet murmur of a fountain placed strategically between two rows of stairs leading to the water completes this balanced, mature landscape whose connection to the past fades as one studies the grouping as a whole.

The visual center of this project is the low sculptured wall that encloses the pool and also provides a means of entering the water. In addition to visually isolating the pool from the more wooded area of the garden, its texture and a fountain that stands at one end constitute an original way to formally balance a narrow, long pool.

This visual expedient, together with the studied landscaping, has softened the pool's strong linearity. In fact, just a glance away lie two soft patches of grass serenely surrounding the pool, countering its hardness. The different tones of the nearby vegetation and the colorful presence of a magnificent bougainvillea, which covers the porch of the house, are the elements that visually order the natural setting, making it a self-contained, easily-maintained garden.

INSPIRED BY THE PAST

Location: **Majorca, Spain**
Surface area: **408 sq. ft.**

The linearity of this pool, shaped like a narrow rectangle, is softened by two grassy slopes covered with easily-maintained vegetation. As the only note of color, a magnificent bougainvillea graces the porch adjacent to the pool.

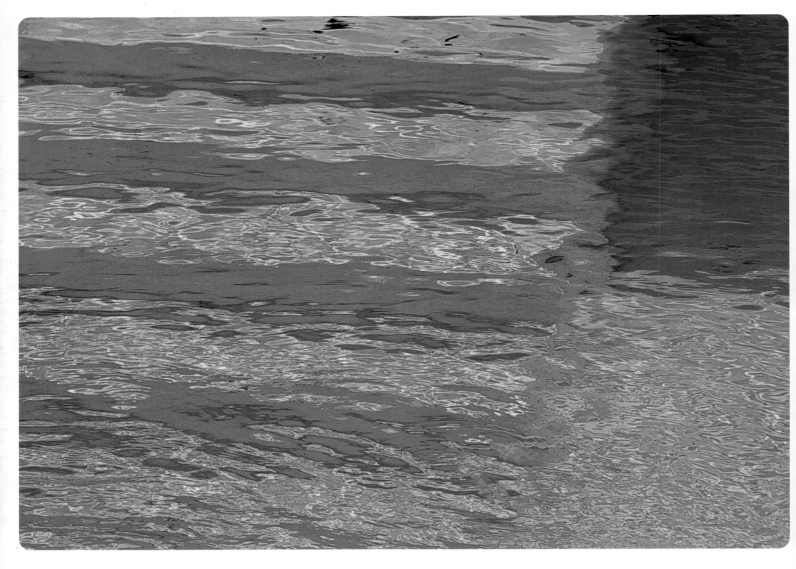

Melting into the immense horizon on this island is not just a privilege, but a singular tribute to its natural beauty.

THE MAGIC OF A SETTING

Location: **Ibiza, Spain**
Surface area: **322 sq. ft.**

Through the use of carefully-placed gradients, a linear geometry that creates spectacular perspectives, and a palette of just one color, blue, a magnificent composition has been achieved that seems to extend visually to the depths of the sea and the heights of the sky.

One of the keys to the grouping is the exterior profile of the swimming pool, which seems to be on the same level as the sea. To enhance this effect, the interior of the pool has been painted white, increasing the contrast of tones while creating a white geometric border, an optical interlude between the intense blue of the sea and the crystalline hues of the pool water.

The simple lines of the two patios next to the pool, combined with the use of unusual materials such as cement, which crowns the pool and covers its entire perimeter, and iron, which acts as the principal support of the exterior structure, are the key elements to the pool's integration with its surroundings. Actually, the use of these two construction materials makes it possible to introduce new textures while still conceding the starring role to the majesty of the landscape and adding character to this unique grouping.

The furniture design is based on the same principle: intelligent ideas and innovative materials for outdoor furniture that has a distinctive style.

The pool features two levels of water in the shape of a "Z," whose exterior perimeter stretches out spectacularly over the bay. Seen from the patio and due to a barely-perceptible gradient, the turquoise water seems to blend with the immensity of the Mediterranean Sea.

Innovative materials and furnishings with a contemporary style were chosen for the patio.

At dusk, the colors blend and the textures soften. The pool and patio take on an aura of serenity in perfect harmony with the setting, but always concede the starring role to the beauty of the landscape.

Changing color with the light, the pool merges with the sea. The different textures of the water, in constant motion, create moments of incredible beauty, as if it were a spectacular kaleidoscope.

This pool is situated in an old, restored Mexican ranch and can be viewed from multiple visual perspectives. Located in the house's uncovered patio, it was conceived as a small, cistern-like pool, inspired by old-fashioned wash-houses. Symmetrically aligned, six jets circulate the water and create a pleasing, natural melody that can be heard from any corner.

In this project, space, color, and the texture of a single material, concrete, merge and complement each other to create a setting rich in nuances, where the light participates directly in creating volumes and perspective. In fact, the forcefulness of the color serves a dual purpose here: to soften the sober quality of the area and to visually lower the height of the room, creating a cool place of refuge from the summer heat. An intense earth color, a warm orange-like tone that stands out in clear contrast to the blue, was chosen for the floor.

For decoration, both the furnishings and ornamental elements were carefully chosen to serve as sculptures. A collection of small bronze statues at strategic locations around the pool, a painting subtly placed at one of the ends, an old swinging bench on the upper level, and even a group of ferns acquire a special prominence enhanced by the presence of color. Finally, a delicate white dove crowns this beautiful composition, a symbol of peace that, in and of itself, conveys the character of this room.

CHROMATIC PERSONALITY

Location: **Jalisco, Mexico**
Surface area: **120 sq. ft.**

An etched glass door separates the pool, located in the semi-covered central patio, from the luminous interior of the house. The colorful contrasts and informal balance can be appreciated from the threshold of the entryway.

The pool, painted an intense indigo blue, was constructed with concrete, the same material that covers the floor, which is painted in earth tone. The floor is easy to maintain and water-resistant, since the patio area is semi-covered.

A row of six slender jets circulate the water in the pool, creating a bright and colorful cascade, which can be heard from almost anywhere in the house.

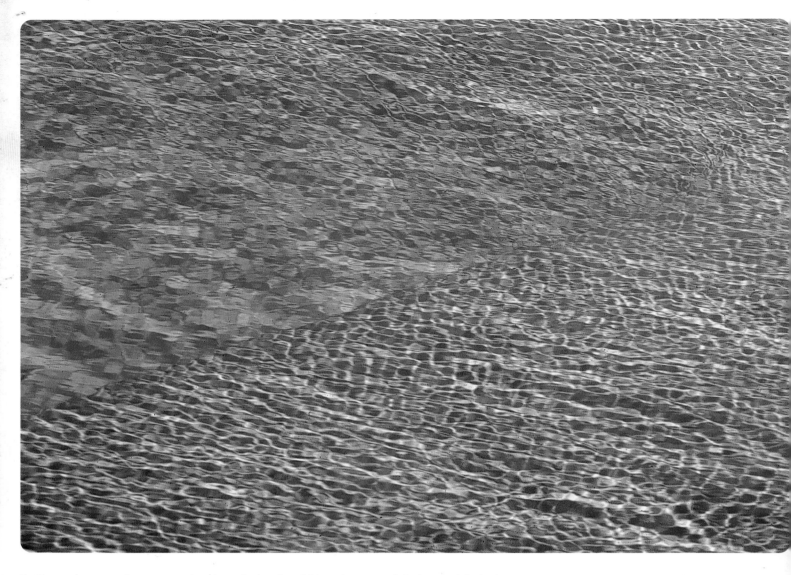

Peeking out from a small, steep cove, the spectacular location of this pool captures all the beauty of the landscape.

Its irregular, wedge-shaped perimeter, with soft, unusual curves, stops at the edge of a cliff, and accommodates three different levels. At the sharpest bend, a first step facilitates entry into the pool. A second skirts the side and forms a kind of underwater bench for relaxing, and the deepest part is at yet a third level.

A single material with a typically Mediterranean texture and tonality, lime cement, was used inside the pool and the area surrounding it. The pines are also typically Mediterranean providing the only note of greenery in this universe of dazzling luminosity.

The design of the pool, built without ornamental trim but with rounded edges, is more about aesthetics and leisure than swimming. Admiring the scenery is paramount, albeit comfortably settled in the water.

This beautiful and powerful landscape seems to be in constant motion, subject to the will of the light. The pool becomes a unique, serene vantage point from which to contemplate, at any time of day, the play and subtle changes of light, a privilege by any standard.

Vantage Point

Location: **Santorini, Greece**
Surface area: **130 sq. ft.**

The pool's exceptional location makes it possible to enjoy the sunsets from a unique vantage point.

The pines provide a note of color in this composition dominated by white and blue.

The immensity of the sea and the endlessness of the landscape can be enjoyed from any of the pool's three levels.

This unique pool is hidden away in the rocky wall of an old quarry high on a hill. To obtain the perfect fusion of the pool and its setting, a natural recess in the rocky wall was used. The result is spectacular: an imposing wall of rock, softened on one side by water from an artificial waterfall and covered on the other side by a blanket of plant life that softens the roughness of the stone.

The pool was treated like a sheet of water, although it resembles the small, deep, natural rock ponds in the eastern part of the Alps, where the water stays frozen even at the height of summer. The rocky wall, including the submerged area, was kept practically intact,

IN THE HEART OF A QUARRY

respecting its structure and unmistakable text- ure. The entrance to the pool reveals, in detail, the merging of the rocky wall with the pool.

Levels and gradients structure the placement of two extensive terraces paved with fired clay flagstones whose reddish color adds a note of warmth while high-lighting the contrast with the light color of the rock. The simplicity of the natural materials enhances the rustic effect of the grouping, although it is softened by the sophisticated iron sun loungers and the elegant color of the upholstered cushions.

Location: **Barcelona, Spain**
Surface area: **215 sq. ft.**

A spectacular view of the pool and lower terrace. The shape of the old stone quarry, now a luxuriant garden, can still be seen amid the thick vegetation.

The rocky wall was kept practically intact, respecting its natural form. The merging of the rocky wall with the volume of the pool can be seen in detail at the pool's entrance.

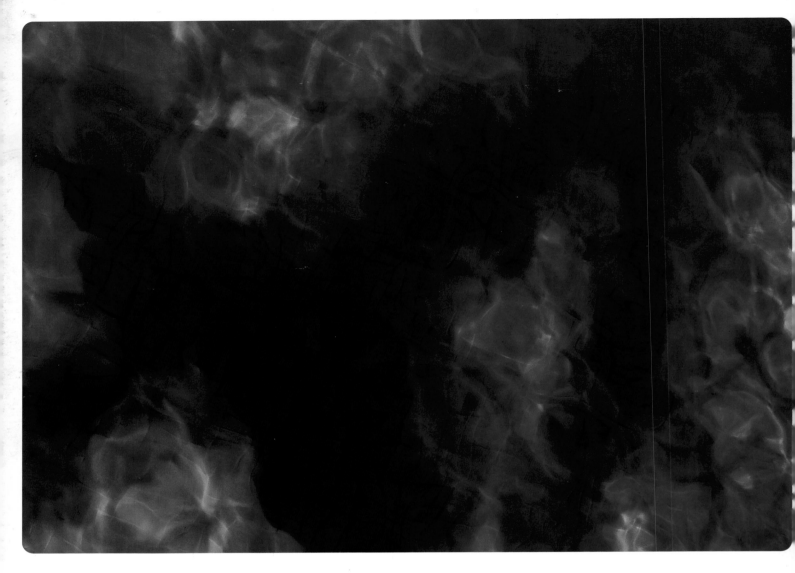

This serene pool rests in a deck of tropical wood that is flush against the rear façade of the house. The formal highly-stylized project places the pool on the same level as the thick blanket of grass that covers the entire garden and was built around the use of three intense colors—organic green, deep blue, and honey brown.

Constructed with Mediterranean-blue gresite and finished inside with the same wood that covers the area, the pool has an entrance that is visually separated from the composition in order to break the pool's rectangular line. The tropical wood deck that shelters the water and covers the entire outdoor patio imparts a sensation of visual dynamism and a touch of velvety warmth.

To unify the materials and textures, the wall dividing this property from the neighbors was designed with the same tropical wood used for the deck and the roof of the pavilion, which was built as an outdoor patio. For this protected and private space, stylized sofas and a table made of iron were chosen, as well as tropical wood sun loungers in a slightly more rustic style.

A thin steel rail visually unites the furniture with the interior bay window at the corner of the house and separates the outside patio from the façade of the house.

ZEN
SYMMETRY

Location: **Barcelona, Spain**
Surface area: **270 sq. ft.**

A wide view of the pool and outdoor patio, which is sheltered by a minimalist pavilion. The tropical wood gives the setting a touch of visual dynamism and integrates the pool and patio.

For this project, a more typical edging was rejected in order to visually integrate the pool area with the tropical wood deck. From this angle, one can see the solution to the problem of the interior finish of the pool's edge.

This magnificent trapezoidal pool is surrounded by a spectacular deck of tonka bean tree wood. Situated next to the main building—a country house—this area was designed and visually linked to the adjacent building by a tropical wood deck in an intense brown color.

The restoration of the country house, the construction of the pool, and the reclamation of a secondary building area occurred in stages over a period of more than five years. To be precise, the entire area was planned in one of the last phases, when the owners bought the adjacent property, which now houses a complete leisure area with a Finnish sauna, a Turkish bath, and changing rooms situated under an impressive arch that reaches up to the ceiling of the old building. A hot tub, strategically placed to take advantage of views of the Ampurdan landscape, completes this balanced, oversized room whose refined style harmonizes different textures: stone, etched glass, and tropical wood.

Outside, a wall of varying heights, perfectly restored and crowned with a bright, tapestry of vegetation, surrounds and protects the area and creates an intimate, cozy space. Moreover, the intelligent combination of colors and textures, including the green of the vegetation, the pale ocher of the stone, and the nat- ural color of the tonka bean tree wood deck, enhances the natural contrasts that make the pool design a splendid exercise in integrating landscape and architecture.

EXERCISE IN CONTRASTS

Location: **Girona, Spain**
Surface area: **484 sq. ft.**

A wall of varying heights, in conjunction with a dense, colorful layer of vegetation, creates a private and cozy space.

Tonka bean tree wood was chosen for the deck around the pool. The wood enhances the natural materials around the pool, such as the stone wall.

The beautiful Ampurdan landscape can be enjoyed from the hot tub.

A sauna and Turkish bath are situated under an impressive arch that reaches up to the ceiling.

The passage of time has left its patina on this complex landscape composition, to which the pool is a worthy addition. The presence of many ponds, parterres, and beautifully paved paths that lead its visitors around the garden, make the pool a secondary but perfectly inte- grated element of this kaleidoscope of plant life.

Surrounding the pool area are several pavilions, whitewashed and coated with a layer of lime mortar. These small structures provide the only note of color in a composition featuring earth tones and an extensive range of greens. Amid the columns, custom-made benches provide a place to chat in the shade. The inside of the pool, also whitewashed, enhances the continuity of the materials and the colors of the setting.

The surrounding area is organized around a low gar-

den that includes papyrus, which grows in the ponds, and cyca, a very slow-growing Japanese species. The plants are combined with various trees, including ancient olive trees, which preside over the entrance to the pool area. In this composition, the vegetation has been sculpted, modeled, and dominated by the hand of man, transformed according to his concept of beauty.

Located on an upper level, separated from the garden by a dividing wall, is an orchard of fruit trees on a carpet of grass. The distribution of the different garden areas, the constant presence of water, and the serene meandering of the paths, were inspired by cloister orchards and gardens.

THE PATINA OP TIME

Location: **Ibiza, Spain**
Surface area: **516 sq. ft.**

On a level above the pool, set apart by a low wall, is a row of vines that lead to an orchard of fruit trees. At the back, a restored stone hut coated with a layer of lime mortar houses the garden tools.

A cloister's orchards and gardens inspired the constant presence of water and the serene character of the paths.

Two plant species are prominent in this garden setting: papyrus, which grows in the ponds, and cyca, a very slow-growing species.

The columns of this pavilion, with custom-made benches where guests can enjoy the shade, frame the pool and afford a beautiful view of the surroundings.

The well is still used by the owners of the house.

A square fountain is the visual center where the garden and main path begin. The path leads to the pool and to the pavilion.

This pool's layout follows the model of the classical houses of Provence, with two clearly differentiated exterior spaces. Situated opposite the house's rear façade, directly in front of the main rooms in order to facilitate direct access, this delicious pool area is well-defined and clearly organized, starting with the various hedges that stretch out in succession from the façade.

On one level is the pool, peaceful, welcoming, and classic, with a subtle elegance that only the passage of time and the hand of an expert gardener can achieve. It is finished with a rustic crown of natural stone, and the inside is coated with blue gresite. Large slabs of unglazed, fired clay pave this recreational area, adding a warm chromatic note and ensuring easy maintenance year round.

This pool's enchanting character is mainly the result of the deliberate, studied, French-style landscaping. The garden, conceived as a natural extension of the house, maintains a delicate symmetry of plant life. Boxwood hedges of different heights visually separate the various landscaped areas. A hammock, the only informal element in this composition, hangs from a refined, stylized, solid wooden structure, which also supports a thick, climbing rose bush, making it a focal point of the area.

Opposite the house, in the landscaped area, sits a small, ancient stone cistern for collecting rainwater. The presence of this beautiful cistern emphasizes the personality and style of the property.

CLASSICAL PERSONALITY

Location: **Les Beaux de Pce., France**
Surface area: **344 sq. ft.**

The pool can be accessed from the main rooms of the house through quaint landscaped parterres that form a path parallel to the rear façade.

Opposite the main entrance, a beautiful, ancient, solid stone water fountain sits next to a small cistern for collecting rainwater.

This spectacular project started with a few ruins, now formally integrated into the pool area. The recovery and reinterpretation of ancient construction methods is an outgrowth of the traditional habitat, based on one ma- terial, earth, and one process, adobe, which involves building with bricks made of earth mixed with straw and dried in the sun.

Used by humans for approximately 10,000 years to build houses and cities, adobe is enjoying a strong resurgence because it is environmentally friendly and insulating, keeping the structure cool in summer and warm in winter in a totally natural manner. Nevertheless, the resurgence of adobe architecture stems not just from interest in the tradition, but also from the very modern concern for the ecology.

For this project, located in a Moroccan paradise—the Marrakech palm grove—a group of ancient ruins was converted into an evocative sculpture, perfectly integrated with the setting and the pool.

The walls were restored with adobe brick, then covered by hand with unbaked adobe, and finally coated with plant oils for protection and preservation.

A pavilion designed in a restrained style presides over the pool, chromatically united with the grouping through an intense ocher, the color of earth, that is also present in the coating of the walls.

THE VALUE OF THE PAST

Location: **Marrakech, Morocco**
Surface area: **485 sq. ft.**

A wide view of the pool, showing the unique overflowing effect. This pool is part of a series of discontinuous levels centered around a group of ancient ruins, now restored and integrated into the project.

A detail of the sophisticated ornamentation decorating the base of the entrance to the pool. The walls are covered with adobe applied by hand and coated with plant oils for protection and preservation.

A pavilion presides over the pool, chromatically united with the grouping by an intense ocher, the color of earth.

A look at the special texture of the hand-applied adobe.

Despite its apparent symmetry, this project on the island of Majorca keeps with the criteria of oriental architecture, based on discontinuity, broken lines, and the lack of a single focal point.

Flanked by majestic palm trees, this swimming pool's edges are elegantly submerged in the water. To the right and on the same level as the still surface of the water, a small square building with a vaulted roof, fronted by a refined porch, rises up like a burst of color. It is an amazing hammam, whose interior, in the shape of an octagonal star, follows the guidelines of Middle Eastern symbolic geometry. Two colors, purplish-blue and soft ocher, dominate the room and filter the sun's luminosity,

inviting one to remain under its intimate protection.

Opposite, a second structure demands attention: erected with strong posts, a large jaima, or traditional Berber tent, designed in the purest Middle Eastern style. Also situated on the same level as the water, its imposing presence is accompanied by a new element, the dry sound of the wind whipping the fabric.

Exotic shapes and unusual textures are combined in this unique project, where space and architectonic rhythm acquire a dimension based on the most subtle emotions and senses.

NOMADIC SENSATIONS

Location: **Majorca, Spain**
Surface area: **483 sq. ft.**

Despite its square exterior shape, the interior of this amazing *hammam* follows the guidelines of Middle Eastern symbolic geometry and is shaped like an octagonal star. Water as a source of life and wealth is the great central character of this unique project.

The presence of a *jaima* with harmonic proportions, fixed with solid posts reaching down to the water, introduces a new element to the pool area: the sound of the wind hitting the fabric.

A side view of the porch and façade. The magnificent, soft ocher *hammam* is hidden behind the façade.

A detail of the underwater steps. The exceptionally wide steps, in combination with the slightly sloped, submerged pool edge, provide a touch of restrained elegance. The color of the outer perimeter was selected to blend with the ocher tones of the *hammam*'s walls.

This *hammam* is sophisticated, but follows traditional patterns. A continuous, balanced series of arches defines the different spaces, united by one color, a soft ocher, and one material, marble, used on the floor and on the tall baseboards. Nooks and crannies create different sitting areas, as required by the rules of the *hammam*, and make it possible to enjoy the art of conversation with a certain discretion and privacy.

Finishing off the marble baseboard, a stylized geometrical border in tricolored ceramic breaks up the chromatic homogeneity, along with indirect light from the transoms, skylights, and windows in the different rooms. The communal water area is square in design, with benches submerged in the cold water. In the differ-

ent rooms of the *hammam*, the wood and brass receptacles, which contain cold water to refresh the user, are the only objects that have not been built into the space, due to the need to replace the water regularly.

Finally, and as required by tradition, one can savor a delicious mint tea and enjoy a few minutes of peace in the sitting room adjacent to the *hammam*, with views of a magnificent enclosed garden. In this room, the ceiling is lined with laurel wood colored with natural pigments, handcrafted using an ancient pre-Saharan technique, and the floor is covered with traditional Moroccan decorative shapes and colors.

SENSORIAL SPACE

Location: Douar Abiat, Morocco
Surface area: **100 sq. ft.**

A continuous, balanced series of arches define the different spaces, finished in a soft ocher.

Niches provide areas where one can sit and enjoy conversation with discretion and privacy.

The magnificent enclosed garden, connected to the sitting room that adjoins the *hammam*. The superb studded door is made of hundred-year-old wood with a finely-carved frame.

In the sitting room adjacent to the water area, where one can go to relax, the ceiling is lined with laurel wood handcrafted using an ancient pre-Saharan technique.

Hidden under a thick climbing plant, a hundred-year-old-wooden door leads us to a refined hammam where the materials take the spotlight. Stone, wood, and an intense blue gresite with flecks of gold, combine to create a charming space.

An old building, where years ago the peasants of Majorca kept their farming tools, was chosen as the location for this small oasis. Vestiges of the building's past have been integrated into the space as benches or towel racks. But the most spectacular part of this project is the perfect combination of the original stone structure and the vibrant color of the floor. This intense contrast has made it possible to integrate the small interior pool and the central channel without visually altering the surface of the floor.

A prominent feature is the small central channel that continues visually in a vertical fashion on the thick stone wall, creating an effect of the side walls coming together. The same effect is achieved by the double play of light, one natural and the other artificial and underwater, between both surfaces.

The walls, more than three feet thick, support a vaulted ceiling, from which the droplets from the dense steam slide down. Two rustic benches and a simple wooden bar for a towel complete the serene setting, conducive to relaxation, where the ritual of water and steam constitute the authentic essence of hammam.

EASTERN

ESSENCE

Location: **Majorca, Spain**
Surface area: **64 sq. ft.**

A small channel of water bisects the central part of the room, creating a visual union of the walls.

The thickness of the walls keeps the *hammam's* interior hot. The vaulted ceiling enables the water droplets produced by the steam to slide down to the floor.

Equipment that was previously used for agricultural work has been recycled to decorate the room.

A point of light placed strategically in the water of the small channel, just below the fixture on the wall, resembles a shaft of sunlight.

The two rustic benches and the various wooden accessories were recovered from the farming-equipment that was once stored in this old building.

Pool Designers:

Eli Mouyal (Pool in introduction)
Wolf Siegfried Wagner (*A Mirror Between the Earth and Sky*)
Tomas Wegner (*Inspired by the Past*)
B&B W Estudio de arquitectura. Sergi Bastidas, Wolf Siegfried Wagner (*Color Contrasts*)
B&B W Estudio de arquitectura. Sergi Bastidas, Wolf Siegfried Wagner (*Nomadic Sensations*)
B&B W Estudio de arquitectura. Sergi Bastidas, Wolf Siegfried Wagner (*The Eternal Cycle of Water*)
Marco Emili (*The Color Turquoise*)
Ramon Esteve, architect (*The Magic of a Setting*)
Juan de los Ríos, architect (*A Stream Amid the Rocks*)
Erwin Bechtold (*Private Space*)
Christopher Travena (*Rural Symmetry*)
Rolf Blackstad, architect (*The Patina of Time*)
Françoise Pialoux (*Vantage Point*)
Bruno, Alexandre & Dominique Lafourcade (*Classical Spirit*)
Guillem Mas, engineer (*Between Two Worlds*)
Aranda, Pigem, Vilalta Arquitectes (*Minimalist Character*)
Tomas Wegner (*Eastern Essence*)
Bruno, Alexandre & Dominique Lafourcade (*Classical Personality*)
Bruno Lafforgue (*Carved in Stone*)
Patrick Genard, architect (*Exercise in Contrasts*)
Àngels G. Giró & Luis Vidal (*Chromatic Personality*)
Lluís Alonso and Sergi Balaguer Arquitectos Asociados (design), XYZ Piscinas (project) (*Zen Symmetry*)
Charles Boccara, architect (*The Reinterpretation of Water*)
Guillermo Maluenda Colomer, architect (*In the Heart of a Quarry*)
Josep Armenter i Arimany, technical architect and coordination
Charles Boccara, architect (*Traditional Inspiration*)
Charles Boccara, architect (*In the Shade of a Palm Grove*)
Charles Boccara, architect (*The Value of the Past*)
Charles Boccara, architect (*Sensorial Space*)
Víctor Espósito (*Textures and forms,* on this page)

The authors would like to give special thanks to the home owners for opening their doors, to the architects for their creativity, and to the following people and groups for their help and collaboration during the development of the stories:

Rafael Calparsoro, Xavier Farré, José Gandia, Nona von Haeften, Laure Jakobiack, Gabriel Vicens and Mamen Zotes, Jean Paul Lance & Jalal Alwidadi, Olivia Vidal & Mercedes Echevarria, Unicorn and Coconut Company(Mallorca. Spain), Gandia Blasco SA(Valencia, Spain), Hotel Les Terrasses (Ibiza, Spain), Hotel Lindos Huéspedes (Pals, Spain), Mas de l'Ange (Mollégés, France), Hotel Les Deux Tours (Marrakech, Morocco).

And:
Antonia & Tomeu, Christian, Bern, Alexandra, Cecilia, Bernadette, Maria, Carmen & Manolo, Nuria, Olivier, Carlos, Danielle & Susan, Said, Aicha, Mohamed, Nassima, Chris, Clay & Annie, Nora, Stanislas.